Blind Moon

Blind Moon

by

Chenjerai Hove

WEAVER
W
—PRESS—

Published by Weaver Press,

Box A1922, Avondale, Harare. 2003.

Cover Design and Typeset by Fontline Electronic
Publishing, Harare

Printed by Mazongororo Paper Converters, Harare

The editor and the publisher would like to express
their gratitude to Hivos for the support they have
given to Weaver Press in the development of their
fiction programme.

ISBN: 1 77922 019 7

contents

Chenjerai Hove was born in Mazvihwa communals lands, southern Zimbabwe, near the mining town of Zvishavane. Novelist, poet, essayist and lecturer, his published fiction includes *Masimba Avanhu?*(1986), *Bones* (winner of the Zimbabwe literary prize in 1988, and the 1989 Noma Award for publishing in Africa), *Shadows*, (1991), and *Ancestors* (1994). His non-fiction work includes *Shebeen Tales* (essays, 1994), *Guardians of the Soil* (with Iliya Trojanow, 1997), *Palaver Finish* (essays, 2002). His poetry includes *Up in Arms* (1982), *Swimming in Floods of Tears* (with Lyamba wa Kabika, 1983), *Red Hills of Home* (1985), and *Rainbows in the Dust* (1997).

He has travelled extensively throughout Africa, Europe, and the United States on lecture tours, and has acted as writer-in-residence at the universities of Zimbabwe, Leeds, Lewis and Clark (Oregon) and Leiden. He is currently living in Rambouillet, France – writing, lecturing and giving poetry readings.

Hove's books have been translated into several languages, including French, German, Japanese, Norwegian, Swedish, Dutch, and Danish.

why poetry?

poetry is a way of laughing and crying. humanity is a queer mixture of laughter and sorrow. it is in the songs and dances of my birth that i drink the waters of poetry.

for, the shona people always say, 'a man without the gift of words will die a bachelor'.

what it means is that poetry is an art to persuade the heart and the soul and human body to be together and to gently cry out to the world.

what is the world? the world has a centre. and everyone is the centre of the world. that is what poetry says to everyone of us. the world is the leaf that is floating in the wind next to me. the task of the poet is to tell the story of how that leaf is floating in the sky with his or her heart also.

the sky? yes. it is in poetry that the human soul can fly and the sky is not even there. poetry allows me to go beyond the sky. poetry is the vehicle of dreams that we ignore all the time.

i used to dream that i was flying. and my father used to think that i needed a traditional healer to cure me of that. i refused the attention of the healer. young as i was, i said, 'why should i not dream like that? it is so beautiful to fly'.

the borders of human geography are broken only when poetry speaks. and poetry speaks not only about landscapes, but about peoplescapes, the human body and its aspirations to be something else. the human soul and its dreams be all the souls of animals and birds and the winds and the skies.

life is like that. and life is poetry.

there is a voice in each one of us. it is silent and deep. but sometimes most of us forget to listen to it. this is where poetry comes in, to allow that suppressed voice to live, to breathe, to fly and be heard.

the forest moves. and what makes it move is the imagination, the poetry, the heart that is always beating inside us all even after we are dead.

did i talk of death? there is nothing like that in poetry. i write poetry in order to refuse death. for, death is also part of life. to die is to live and to live is to die.

then poetry becomes a celebration of the complex mixture of the living and the dead.

in poetry, i am part of other voices in other hearts, but i am also part of the voices that are ignored. the voices of the insects, th e birds, the sky, the soil and the air we breath.

i write poetry to search for my voice and its destiny, and also to search for the voices of others and their destiny. because by being born, we are launched into the space of life, but life itself is a search for a destiny, a search for destinies and possibilities.

when everything else is silent, poetry speaks to my heart and yours. and the world becomes one solid piece of mind and heart.

chenjerai hove

when the sky is clear

i wish i were a bird,
flying,
a bird with wings.

no one loves
a bird with a broken wing.

when the sky is clear
i wish i were a bird
flying
with outstretched wings.

no one loves
a bird with a broken wing.

butterfly

now i know
i am alone;

the cloud,
my only friend,
still drifts away
when i want to touch her thighs.

i am alone
and commitments take you away
like a butterfly with sticky wings
flying flying flying
afraid to perch.

flying away

from me.

birds

i am watching the sky,
the clouds,
birds printing only their destiny,
not mine,
in the shape of wings.

where are my wings?

tree

i saw a tree
without a shadow;

history writes itself
on leaves
and blank spaces.

pain

there is a pain
i cannot name,
inside me.
there is a painless pain
that refuses to be named.

there is a shapeless pain
inside me.

there is a painful piece of land
inside me,
a pain without a name,
inside me.

trail

on your way
to the house of power
you left footprints of blood
so many broken hearts
so many broken brains
so many broken bricks.

on your way
to the house of power
you left an endless trail of blood.

on your way
to the house of power
you left a trail of orphans
you left a trail of widows
you left a trail
of pain.
you devoured the colour
of our gentle hearts.

on your way
to the house of power
you left a trail

of unsmiling faces,
of broken skulls
and nameless graves.

days do not smile
on those who sup on human blood,
suns do not rise
for those who wield only death.
the moon too,
changes its colour
to this dark red,
clotting on the pavements of conscience.

on your way
to the house of power
you left too many scars,
you wounded even the trees,
the birds,
our butterflies of hope,
on your way
to the house without a sky
and boundless power.

the birds went silent
afraid to sing of their freedom;

their eggs were broken,
and the waterpot too,
broken on the trail of power.

on your way
to the house of power
you left puddles of tears;
on your way to the house of mirages,
the house of boundless power,
you left us forever
with only two fingers
and wells of tears
all drained to emptiness.

on your way
to the house of power
you refused to listen
to the tunes of birds:
the birds of your conscience.

sky

i am here
under the same sky
as you
i am here
wielding the same shadow
as you

i am here
where you are
under the same sky.

to a dictator

in your time
you took away
the flowers of our freedom.
in your time
the weak defended
your weakness,
and the land cried;
the moon too
was dark
in your time.

(in memory of a pakistani poet who refused)

cap

who is wearing who,
the cap or you?

give the cap freedom
in a reckless dance,
and let the eagle perch
on that shaven head.

for charles mungoshi

13

african farmer's son in europe

it rained all day,
and the french curse the rain;
every raindrop of it
evokes ten raindrops
in curses.

i, annoyed,
think i should farm.

i buy first priority
the plant pots,
then in amazement,
i wander the streets
searching for the soil.

it takes all day
to buy a bit of soil.

that done,
ah, jesus, son of joseph,
i pick up the phone:
the plant man has a late lunch.

the manure man is on strike
against increased prices of toothpaste.

everything is green around,
they say to me.

except me,
i interject.

the rains still fall
in front of a farmer's son,
in europe
where rains disturb the peace.

at least i will grow
and grow a tomato,
for the sake of faith
in the soil.

onion

only one onion left
between now and tomorrow,
between my departure
and my arrival.

there is only one onion left,
between two pieces of history,
between this departure
and the next unknown destination.

in rambouillet, france

there is the woman,
the one everyone knows is crazy,
the one who kisses the chateau
and urinates on the flowers.

there is a young man too,
who speaks no word
and shakes everyone's hand;

they say he too is mad,
with no fixed abode.

everyone looks the other way
when a bad smell traverses these parts,
for the sake of peace
and a painted vegetable conscience.

moon

when the moon comes out
i will not think of you,

i will know you.

graffiti

a child's finger
another death
no tears
mother is out of this space
we can see from the pathprints

father only whispered his death wish
to armed men.

graffiti
on the wall of the sky.

we

we were not
the only ones left;
the fig-tree stood by us.

we were not
the only ones left
until the sky refused us
a visa.

sweet dreams, dear
as we wait
for another flower to bloom.

misty

i feel
you are part of a raindrop,
and i am part
of the mist.

all visions
sometimes obscure in doubt
till the final penalty.

love

you took away
our only moonlight,
that moon of love.

you planted anger
in our hearts.

you took away
the burning petals
of our new moon.

may the earth swallow you
without chewing,
without tears.

peeping

someone is peeping
at the corners of my mind
in secret.

someone is peeping
at my soul,
the only remnant of me
in this fog.

encounter

a woman in tight shorts
stocky
walks
and touches the gravestones.

what you is doing? she asks me.
just looking at the graves, i say.
you work here? i ask.
no, watching the graves, she spits,
and leaves.

we part
    she, touching the graves
    me, watching the graves.

both of us vandals.

marson's bar, doncaster, 1995

the general sips his whiskey,
smells the wild scent of the girls,
sips again
to his heart's content;
all the lads praise him:
monsieur generale!
monsieur generale!

they praise him,
their words echoless
in marson's bar.

the market women sell fish outside
and the corn merchants shout prices,
their pale thirst yielding to lower prices.

years later, sun upon sun,
the general's blood appears
in the shape of a great-great-granddaughter.

my great-great-grandfather's underpants,
she says.

he drank here
and made love to the market woman.

the bartender yells
but the ancestors know the story
of love and medals and underpants.

this bar made the war effort,
soldiers drank here
on their way to napoleonic wars,
the wall plaque says.

monsieur generale!
monsieur generale!
your french needs shape
the drunken soldier says
as the general goes to the toilet.

memory

i will remember you
for not remembering anything;
even the flowers under your pillow
were not anything to remember.

i will remember you
for not remembering anything.

even the baby on your back
was not worth remembering.

i will remember you
for not remembering.

what are you doing?

when streams of children's blood
creep on your desks, mournfully;
when mothers only have memories for
husbands;
what are you doing?

raindrops of tears on your table,
tears of zimbabwean mothers,
children!
fathers,
searching for the disappeared.

procedure!
procedure!
you shout
in eloquent french
and immaculate suits.

and the land overflows with despair.

what are you doing
when every hill harbours a political corpse
when the teachers' pillows are fresh skulls
and villagers sing songs at gunpoint?

what are you doing

when only praise-singers eat and laugh

when the hills are places of fear

when the soil smells of fresh blood and
corpses?

what are you doing

when civil war reigns

when spears are sharpened

when guns run the household

in the hands of the rulers ?

what are you doing

when the teacher's bare buttocks

are exposed in front of the school parade

when lady teacher is raped

in front of the children she teaches?

what are you doing

smiling, drinking good german wine,

debating outcomes already there,

when the sun rises only for the rulers

and the earth trembles in front of children's
small feet ?

what are you doing

when tyranny eats at the skin of defenceless

people

when tyranny devours its own people

and drenches its mouth

with the blood of the citizens ?

you may not remember me,

but i am the child

who knocks on the door of your conscience

every morning at your breakfast of juicy
steaks

and a dash of ice cream.

i am only a tiny grain

of the memory you abandoned.

you will not hear me soon,

for i will only be a pool of silence:

dead or raped to silence.

what are you doing

when the republic is burnt to ashes

by those entrusted with hands of morality ?

the joyful songs die

from lips that starve.

the birds that sing
are shot dead
and the militia determine
the red colour of the sky.
village kings kneel
to the murderers
in prayer to be spared another death.
what are you doing
sitting in your palace
debating stale possibilities
and futile scenarios
while reality stares you in the face
like a starving child ?

i know
you will not remember me
for i am only a blank map
filed by neither you nor god.

blind moon

blind moon,
doomed to see
all these corpses.

blind moon
so blind
doomed to see
all these shadows
of political corpses.

blind moon,
it is better to remain blind.

monkey

now we know
a monkey is a
monkey is a
monkey,
in you.

hope

i think of a leaf
floating   floating   floating
in the wind.

i think of a leaf
        floating

and i think of you
        and me
floating in the wind
floating with the wind

floating   floating   floating
in the wind

not falling.

sunk

our moon was sunk
our sun was sunk
both red with planetary tears,
of blood from our own veins.

help us cry for our moon
help us cry for our sun
help us demand our smiles back.

omen

if you appear again
do not be a star,
be an omen.

search

after the search
there is nothing
except the coffin
and a dying homestead.

kokoriko

the village dies.
a man with money came,
bought the cockerel—
the only one left in the village.

kokoriko is gone—
like the village—
on the ticket of money.

bother

do not bother;
you never bothered anyway,
even when the moon
came to tell you stories,
you never bothered.

this sun is all over.

your sky
my moon
they went in different directions,
as you went to the bank
in search of old bank notes.

when

when your eyes
were there
the moon refused to come out;

shy moon!

eyes with a permanent glow,
give me the landscape
i can only give you the inscape.

slice

i am a slice
of the moon,
you are a slice
of the sun.

mysteries merge
once in many moons.

it is not

it is not that dreams are wild;
it is not that we cannot sleep.
when distances rebel
and faces fade in the dim light of memory,
we stand on stone memory
as the world goes by,

and you cannot hear my silent poems
of yearning never before recorded,
and i cannot hear your silent pulse.

it is not that sounds die
it is not that mountains have no echoes
it is not that we don't fall sometimes.

it is that the echoes of the mountain
merge into one,
and give birth to a hill.

lamb

the day thieves
stole the sacrificial lamb
and the priest was waiting,

then everyone knew
who was in charge
of religious stories,
destinies.

share

let us share
the moon
the sky
the landscape
the bodyscape,

a destiny of stars.

one person

all those eyes
in one person;
all those hearts,
the moons,
the stars
in one face.

maybe i am young again
this summer.

saint malo

a little boy
plays with the sea;
the waves wave
at the little boy,
the water nibbles
at his feet.

far away beyond the seas
a little girl
plays with the sea,
the sea of copacabana embraces her:
the little girl
playing with the sea in rio.

what a distant kiss
in the water
saint malo
rio

love in the water
mailed by the sea waters.

one day the two may meet,
like waters kissing their feet
in love.

rain

there is a raindrop
that i will follow
to the sea,
its shape like a flowery nipple
in the thunder.

flowers

when i die
the last death,
maybe you will send a flower
by dhl
to celebrate,
to know that
once i lived.

all these tears,
a wasteland.

just remember the flowers
by whatever means.

i only write
on a slate of tears
and endless dreams.

remains of the sky

if the sky
still remains the same
we will meet
and pay homage
to ourselves.

if the sky still obeys seasons,
we will be the remains
of another sky.

mandela

i refused to die
before i could write
a tribute to you,
you who gave flowers of the heart
just as others gave bullets
and tears for their inheritance.

mandela,
i refused to die
before this poem
of the flowery mushrooms
you gave to our lands.

those who plant love
harvest only love;
those who plant hatred and bullets
harvest only death.

mandela,
may you pour libation
to your parents
who are now everyone's parents.

you see,

even in the underground in tokyo

their graffiti said it:

free mandela.

the soil

i will cry for you
i will weep for you
i mourn for you before death.

i dig the potato i planted—
it is red with blood.
i dig a well for the children's thirst—
i meet a sky with a bullet hole.

earth of my mothers
earth of my fathers

i cry for you
as i see old men of power
wielding blood-plastered fists,
as i see old women of power
wielding grinding stones made of skulls.

land, i cry for you
as you lose your voice
to the echoes of the sky,
your beauty sinking,
your breath turning into mist,
your vision blurred in the mist.

tomorrow

outside tomorrow
and yesterday
there is still another day
called destiny.

a poem for zimbabwe

i am the only one
you are the only one.

the birds and the rivers
sing to me,
they speak in your voice.

if i fall silent
you will be silent too.
if i fall silent
your wounds will be named silence.

i am a piece of you
and you are a piece of me.

the blood in my veins is you.
listen to the rhythm
of the stream of my blood
and the echoes from the hills,
mixed with gentle ripples
of the waters in the fast stream.

but with time

you will hear your voice

in the blue skies of my heart.

in the dark clouds of my soul

you will hear a voice

that tells the story of your forgotten voices

of birds long dead

of elephants crippled by guns

of orphans you do not deserve.

ahead

from now on
we tread the road,
the footpath of illegitimacy
to the tune
of praise singers
flatterers
charlatans.

one day

one day
when i shall die
only spare
a secret tear for me
in a secret place
without a shadow.